Landscapes of America

First English edition published by Colour Library Books.
© 1983 Illustrations and text: Colour Library International Ltd.
   99 Park Avenue, New York, N.Y. 10016, U.S.A.
This edition is published by Crescent Books
Distributed by Crown Publishers, Inc.
h g f e d c b a
Colour separations by FERCROM, Barcelona, Spain.
Display and text filmsetting by ACESETTERS LTD., Richmond, Surrey, England.
Printed by Cayfosa and bound by Eurobinder - Barcelona (Spain)
ISBN: 0.517.427222
CRESCENT 1983

Dep. Leg. B. 30.820/83

Landscapes of America

Text by Bill Harris

Produced by
TED SMART and DAVID GIBBON

CRESCENT BOOKS

Back in the 1920s when the British writer G.K. Chesterton was planning a trip to the United States, he visited the American Consulate to have his passport brought up to date. One of the questions on the form he was handed was: "Are you in favor of subverting the Government of the United States by force?" His first reaction, he said, was to write: "I intend to subvert the Government of the United States by force as soon as possible by sticking the long sheath-knife in my left trouser pocket into Mr. Harding at the first opportunity." He didn't, of course, and President Harding was spared having another worry added to his troubles. What Chesterton wrote instead was: "I prefer to answer that question at the end of my tour rather than at the beginning."

At the end of the tour he wrote a book. It was called *What I Saw in America.* It was obvious to any reader that if he had ever harbored any subversive thoughts, his trip had subverted them. Though he was clearly not ready to start filling out naturalization papers, he was just as clearly impressed by what he saw. And one of the things that impressed him most was a simple thing: wood.

"I saw forests upon forests of small houses stretching away to the horizon as literal forests do", he wrote. "And they were, in another sense, literally like forests. They were all made of wood. It was almost as fantastic to an English eye as if they had been made of cardboard."

"The houses may look like a gypsy caravan on a heath or common; but they are not on a heath or common. They are on the most productive and prosperous land, perhaps, in the modern world. The wooden houses may fall down like shanties, but the fields would remain; and whoever tills those fields will count for a great deal in the affairs of humanity."

He saw real forests, too, of course. The forest primeval that Longfellow celebrated was, and is, still a place of murmuring pines and hemlocks. And though he saw row on row of freshly built houses behind signs that said "Watch Us Grow", signs which he claimed made one imagine "timbers swelling before his eyes like pumpkins in some super-tropical summer", he saw empty spaces that made growth an understandable dream.

And if he were to take that tour again, now that sixty eventful years have passed, he'd still find a land of forests, open spaces and an incredible variety of natural beauty.

Americans are as proud of their cities as of their natural landscape and there is no denying Chesterton's observation that the electric signs in New York's Times Square would be a glorious garden of wonders to anyone who was lucky enough to be unable to read. But in spite of several generations of homage to the slogan "Watch Us Grow", it's amazing how much open space the builders have missed. On an airline shuttle from Boston to Washington, flying over what may be the most heavily populated corridor in the world, the view from the window is more often of fields and forests than of cities and subdivisions. The view from the Sears Tower in Chicago is more of green than urban grid. And the short ride across San Francisco's Golden Gate Bridge takes you to a virtually untouched area of hillsides and seashore, parts of which could easily make you feel that no other human being has ever set foot there; yet back there over your shoulder is one of the most dramatic panoramas ever created by man; the towers of the city.

In 1981, the population of the U.S. was set at just under 230 million, a density of about 65 people per square mile. They shared the space with just about half that number of cattle, 13 million sheep, 58 million hogs and more than 1.7 chickens for every man, woman and child. The food produced on the land contributed close to $86 billion to the Gross National Product, over $2 billion more than the entire GNP of Saudi Arabia. Yet, of the 3.6 million square miles of area in America, less than 3,000 square miles are divided into farms. By contrast, almost 36,000 square miles are forest land.

This is in spite of the fact that since the time the first Europeans began arriving and setting up colonies along the Eastern Seaboard, getting trees out of their way has been a number one priority. There were wooden houses to be built, as Chesterton noticed, and more wood was needed to keep them warm in winter. There were farms to be cleared and trees needed to be removed to make way for towns. These Europeans cut down trees to make furniture, toys for their children, tools for themselves. The binge hasn't stopped yet. In 1980, Americans consumed nearly 39 billion board feet of lumber, almost 80 million cords of pulpwood. It adds up to just about 69 cubic feet of wood for every person in the United States.

The people who started the ball rolling in the 17th century must have been overwhelmed by the abundance of it all. Their ancestors had long since realized that though trees represent a renewable resource, the supply doesn't exactly come from a bottomless pit. The tradition of knocking on wood for luck had originated with these people who had in mind the wooden cross that Christ had died on and the fact that He had been a carpenter, but they extended the superstition out of respect for what they knew was a rare commodity.

The explorers who preceded them looking for the treasures of the Orient, already knew from Marco Polo's travels that wood was not one of those riches. The very idea behind oriental quick-cooking is based on a wood shortage centuries old that made slow-burning fires a luxury nobody could afford. Of course, men like Columbus would have laughed at the idea that trees might be more valuable than gold and the people who followed him into the New World considered the forests more of a nuisance than a resource. The problem was that they couldn't see the forests for the trees and the trees were in the way of progress.

In the beginning they set about getting rid of the nuisance with time-honored methods of saws and axes. It was slow work. It was hard work. But even the earliest Americans were resourceful people, especially when it came to saving time and work. By the time they began moving into the wilds of Ohio and Indiana, in the years after becoming an independent country, they had devised a new way of clearing land. Once they determined that an area of forest land would be good for farming or pasturage, they simply stripped the bark from all the trees in little bands completely encircling them. Since trees transmit nutrients from leaves to roots through the outer layer of bark, the stripping literally starved them to death. Once dead they were much easier to cut, but most of the farm builders didn't go to all that trouble. Dead trees are easier to burn, too. And that's what they did. Burning eliminated the problem of what to do with all those logs as well, and when a field had been reduced to a bunch of charred stumps, oxen were brought in to get rid of them.

Establishing farms and fields made the landscape all the way from the coast to the Mississippi something different than it had been in the days when Indians roamed unaware that their days were numbered. Today's travellers on Interstate highways and turnpikes between New York and Chicago are largely looking at a man-made countryside even though they pass through many miles of territory that look for all the world as though an Algonquin hunting party would easily recognize the place.

"What hath man wrought?" is a question any traveller crossing the American continent needs to consider. Even most of the untouched places represent the hand of man staying the hands of other men. The Department of the Interior oversees 333 "Park Service Areas", including 48 National Parks that cover more than 44.4 million acres. The National Forest System watches over a total of 230 million acres, 191 million of which are within the boundaries of protected forest land; the balance, also protected, includes grassland and research and experimental areas. In addition, the various states have earmarked 9.3 million acres to remain forever wild and available only for recreation.

The National Park System extends from Acadia, on Mount Desert Island in northern Maine, which includes rocky cliffs and coves, a 1,500-foot pink granite mountain and the only true fjord on the United States Atlantic coast, all the way to Haleakala on the Hawaiian Island of Maui, established on the crater of a dormant volcano that is home to the iiwi bird, whose vermillion feathers were once reserved for the exclusive use of the island's royalty. The system rises above sea level to 20,320 feet at the highest mountain in North America, Alaska's Mount McKinley, in the heart of Denali National Park, and plunges 360 feet below ground to the

Echo River in the depths of Mammoth Cave in Kentucky.

The United States was the first country to establish national parks, an idea that has been copied widely all over the world. But though it's an idea that Americans accept as a part of their heritage, it is one that is only a little more that a century old. And it is an idea that people themselves largely ignored for a generation or more.

The history of the system goes back to 1832 when the mineral springs at Hot Springs, Arkansas, were reserved under Government protection to prevent overdevelopment. Then, in 1864, Congress turned the Yosemite Valley over to the State of California with vague instructions to leave it the way it was. Congress took it back in 1900 at the urging of naturalist John Muir who took a trip there from his home 150 miles away in San Francisco and stayed for 40 years. By that time, Americans had been living with the idea of national parks for 28 years but most of them didn't seem to care all that much.

There was no public hue and cry for the preservation of nature in 1871 when two bills were introduced in Congress to set aside the northwest corner of Wyoming and parts of Idaho and Montana as a "National Park". Both bills were the result of lobbying and arm-twisting by a small group of citizens from that part of the country. The debates didn't attract a whole lot of attention and many who did go to the trouble to read about what was going on agreed with a California Senator who reasoned:
"The natural curiosities there cannot be interfered with by anything that man can do. The geysers will remain no matter where the ownership of the land may be, and I do not know why settlers should be excluded from a tract of land 40 miles square", he was off by 20 miles in each direction, "in the Rocky Mountains or any other place. I cannot see how the natural curiosities can be interfered with if settlers are allowed to appropriate them."

Obviously the Senator didn't understand the nature of people. There are natural wonders all over the United States today; waterfalls, caverns, rock formations, that are located on private property whose owners have turned them into profit centers, charging visitors a fee to have a look. Worse still, they have seen fit to dot the landscape with their tacky billboards to call attention to their natural attractions. And, often as not, once you've paid your money, you'll find the landscape marred with gift shops, picnic groves and parking lots, not to mention the litter that goes with all three.

Such things were foreseen in the Yellowstone debate.

Nobody had experienced the nightmare of a parking lot back in 1871, but the rest of it was reflected in a speech made by a Senator from Illinois as the debate moved along:

"Here is a region of the country way up in the Rocky Mountains where there are the most wonderful geysers on the face of the earth; a country that is not likely ever to be inhabited for the purposes of agriculture; but it is possible that some person may go there and plant himself across the only path that leads to these wonders, and charge every man that passes along between the gorges of these mountains a fee of a dollar or five dollars. He may place an obstruction there, and toll may be gathered from every person who goes to see these wonders of creation."

Fortunately, the Senate version of the bill passed in February 1872 and was signed into law by President Ulysses S. Grant within two days.

Most Americans yawned. And life in the Yellowstone area went on pretty much as it had before the President picked up his pen. The mountain men continued to run their trap lines, the Indians continued giving them a hard time. What few settlers there were continued to eke out an existence and the geyser known as "Old Faithful" continued to erupt every 65 minutes, right on schedule.

A few tourists showed up to have a look around, but all through the 1870s and well into the 80s, getting there was no fun at all.

There were two ways to get to Yellowstone in those days. You could catch a steamboat at Bismarck, North Dakota (and getting **there** was a trip to write home about!) which would take you 400 miles up the Missouri River and then down the Yellowstone River another 360 miles to the Big Horn and 60 miles more to the town of Clark's Fork, Montana where you could switch to a stagecoach bound for Bozeman, Montana. From Bozeman another coach would take you the rest of the way, a mere 72 miles. The uphill thousand-mile trip from Bismarck took about two weeks, but getting back was faster. The round-trip cost a little over $100. For people with a lot more money and a little less time, the Union Pacific Railroad took them from Omaha, Nebraska to Ogden, Utah for a connection with the Utah Northern, which deposited them near the Snake River above Pocatello, Idaho. From there, they faced a 380-mile stagecoach ride to Bozeman and then, before they had time to dust themselves off, another 72-mile trip down into the Park. That trip took 10 days, each way, and cost $200.

Once there, tourists had to contend with hostile Indians, too. Though the Indians themselves generally avoided the area out of fear of the geothermal features they were convinced were the work of evil spirits, they considered it their territory and did all they could to keep the White Man off balance. The problem was finally resolved by treaty in 1880. It was one of the few Indian treaties, incidentally, that worked the first day it was negotiated. Absence of greed was one reason. But those evil spirits did their bit.

But by that time it was apparent that the real menace was not Indians, not grizzly bears, not boiling-hot geysers but the tourists themselves. Elk were gunned down just for their teeth, buffalo for their skulls. Sport fishermen found out they could cut corners and increase their yield by dropping sticks of dynamite into the rivers. The colored borders of geysers and springs were broken apart by souvenir hunters and it was considered great fun to break off tree branches and poke around at the geysers. Not one of them escaped some form of destruction.

Out in California, John Muir, the poet of Yosemite, had some thoughts about thoughtless people who did such things:

"The smallest reserve, and the first ever heard of," he wrote, "was in the Garden of Eden, and though its boundaries were drawn by the Lord, and embraced only one tree, yet the rules were violated by the only two settlers that were permitted on suffrage to live on it."

In spite of the discouraging start, the idea of a National Park system kept smouldering on. Four years after the establishment of Yellowstone, Congress set aside Mackinac Island, off the northern Lake Huron coast of Michigan, as a protected area for "the enjoyment of the people". It was a great idea on paper, but within a dozen years it had become a preserve for "the right kind of people" when an elegant, expensive hotel was built there. A few years later the island was turned over to the state.

The issue of state's rights reared its head just about every time anyone raised the subject of a Federal park. While the basic idea was to protect the landscape from settlement, farming or any other form of alteration, the idea in the minds of most was that such projects would be not only self-supporting, but would earn a tidy profit as well. The Yellowstone experience dashed some of those hopes, but the men in the various State Houses couldn't help smelling an opportunity to make a buck and most were reluctant to let those dollars go to Washington. When it finally became apparent that such parks were expensive to run and not only would never make a profit, but prevented any chance of profiteering on minerals, timber and other natural resources, State Legislatures began supporting the idea of parks administered by the Federal Government. It took time, though. Their constituents still weren't clamoring for parks and the potential for profit in development was awfully tempting.

But the beat went on. The Grand Canyon, many felt, ought to be protected. Timber interests were eyeing the giant sequoias in California and lobbying was started to protect them. But the public eye was on a beautiful valley in California the Indians had named Yosemite; their word for the huge grizzly bears that made their home there.

The bulk of the American population lived on the East Coast in those pre-Civil War days and not many of them had the slightest idea of the wonders of such places as Yosemite. In the 1850s Horace Greeley, the editor of *The New York Tribune,* began telling them. Greeley travelled extensively through the West and never neglected to write home about it. It was he who promulgated the theory that God intended man to tame and settle the West. And it was he who gave the movement a name: "Manifest Destiny". It was also he who upset New York by editorially advising its sons to "go West, young man".

He explored the Yosemite Valley in 1859 and pronounced it "the most majestic of nature's marvels". Among the people he impressed was a young man named Frederick Law Olmstead, a confirmed nature-lover who had a dream of becoming a great landscape architect. Olmstead was so impressed he got out his drawing board and began designing a huge public park. The State of California was so impressed that when the Federal Government turned over the Valley to them in 1864, they put him in charge. After a few months, though, he left California to accept what he considered a better job offer. He had been asked to become the architect of New York City's Central Park.

But he left the Valley in good hands. Naturalist John Muir arrived there less than five years later and picked up where Greeley had left off, writing descriptions of the incredible beauty he found there. "Awful in stern, immovable majesty, how softly these rocks are adorned with a thousand flowers leaning confidingly against their feet, bathed in floods of water", he wrote in Century Magazine and Americans everywhere got the picture. But it took more than 20 years of such writing to get Congress to respond. Muir's campaign was aimed at protecting the area and keeping it forever beautiful, but it wasn't until he zeroed in on a specific aspect of it that he began getting attention in the right places.

Not far south of his beloved valley there are groves of trees so incredible that when a section of one of them was taken to an exhibition in Victorian London, no one would pay to see it because they thought it was a fraud. Nature couldn't possibly have created a tree that big, they said. But nature had. A long time ago. They are called giant sequoias but they make the word "giant" seem like an understatement. Their trunks are up to 35 feet in diameter and they rise more than 270 feet into the air. They've been growing on the west slope of the Sierra Nevada for more than 3,500 years.

In Muir's day there were five sawmills working furiously to undo what nature had taken all that time to create. Even though it took more than three weeks to cut one of the trees down and much of the work had to be done with dynamite; and even though the wood turned out to be useless for most traditional purposes, the loggers were determined to meet the challenge. Muir criticized them by writing: "Waste far exceeds use. For after the young manageable trees have been cut, blasted and sawed, the woods are fired to clear the ground of limbs and refuse, and of course the seedlings and saplings, and many of the unmanageable giants, are destroyed, leaving but little more than black, charred monuments".

The result of such reports finally became a monument to Muir himself. In 1890, 15 years after they created Yellowstone, Congress responded to public pressure by declaring more than 30 groves of giant sequoias as a public park. Five days later they established two more parks, the General Grant sequoia grove and Yosemite. The General Grant grove is now part of the expanded Sequoia National Park; Yosemite, meanwhile, has grown to four times its original size.

After having established three National Parks in a single session, Congress was pleased with itself and lobbyists began egging them on. The most powerful lobby at the time represented the railroad interests and representatives of the Northern Pacific Railroad saw an opportunity in Mount Rainier in Washington. Though there are four higher mountains in the continental United States, Rainier was everybody's favorite, probably because of its graceful symmetry and beautiful setting. Organizations like the Sierra Club and the National Geographic Society had made it famous and were among the first to campaign to have it set aside as a National Park. Commercial interests didn't stand in the way; the mountain was isolated and glacier-covered. The people who lived in the area were enthusiastic about the idea and in 1895 Congress took the matter up. The bill, proposing establishment of "Washington National Park", looked like an easy winner. Then the lobbyists entered the picture. They succeeded in having a rider attached to the bill which would give the right of way into the new Park exclusively to the Northern Pacific and allow the railroad to trade any land it owned on the mountain (and it owned plenty!) for equal amounts of land in any other state where they already had rights of way.

Fortunately, there were some Congressmen the lobbyists had not reached and though the bill was passed, they were able to persuade the President, Grover Cleveland, not to sign it into law.

The railroad got what it wanted, but so did the people. And at least with the railroad behind it, Mount Rainier promised to be more accessible to more people than Yellowstone had been.

Unfortunately, there would soon be a new President and the railroad people didn't give up. A new bill was introduced. It was the same as the first, but the name of the park was changed to make it look different. It passed easily and President McKinley signed the law that created Mount Rainier National Park, the nation's fifth, in 1899.

The 20th century was less than a year old when the country got another new President and this one, Theodore Roosevelt, was passionate about protecting the landscape. His influence encouraged an effort that had been going on since the 1880s to create another park around Crater Lake in Oregon.

The lake, nearly 2000 feet deep and five miles across, fills the crater of a volcano that exploded thousands of years ago. Its depth gives it a blue color that is perfectly complemented by the colored rocks and rich evergreens around it. That, all by itself, made it a candidate for preservation. But though it's the deepest lake in the United States, six others in the world are deeper, and some others may be considered more beautiful, it is the perfect spot for scientists to find out how the mountain was built, how it was destroyed and how the crater was formed.

Like Mount Rainier, the area was considered useless for anything else anyway, and President Roosevelt signed the legislation making Crater Lake a National Park in 1902.

The following year three more parks were established, almost without comment and with very little fanfare. Only one of the three, Wind Cave in the Black Hills of South Dakota, still exists as a National Park although another, Platt National Park in Oklahoma, is still administered by the Park Service. The third, Sully's Hill in North Dakota, officially became a game preserve in the 1930s. Ironically, of the three, Sully's Hill was the only one established without formal Congressional approval. It came into existence on the wings of a proclamation issued by President Roosevelt.

By that point it was clear that of all the areas that needed Federal protection against vandals and developers, many didn't deserve the status of National Park. After a great deal of debate, Congress finally came up with what they called "The Antiquities Act", which was mainly designed to protect archaeological sites. The bill referred to such places as "National Monuments", and when it became law in 1906 the term became part of standard governmentese. They weren't thinking of such things as the Gettysburg battlefield or the Alamo, which is why the first National Monument under the law was Devil's Tower, an 865-foot shaft rising above the flat terrain of Eastern Wyoming.

Teddy Roosevelt seems to have had a good time naming National Monuments during the rest of his term as President. In less than two years he designated 18 of them including the Petrified Forest in Arizona, whose calcified trees and mineral formations were being hauled away by the ton by vandals and souvenir hunters; and Muir Woods, a grove of giant redwoods near San Francisco. He also included a few that would eventually be transformed into National Parks, the Grand Canyon among them.

His successor, William Howard Taft, named another seven before finally designating one that was a "monument" in the real meaning of the word. In 1910, he established the Big Hole National Battlefield, near Butte, Montana.

No one thought this was odd or unusual. While the President had been given the authority to designate National Monuments, Congress had been doing the same thing since 1890 when they began setting aside Civil War battlefields as military parks.

But the President and Congress worked together through those years to establish more National Parks, too. In 1906, President Roosevelt signed the law creating Mesa Verde National Park, a collection of ruins from communities of cliff dwellers who lived in what is now Southwestern Colorado as far back as the first century. In 1910 President Taft authorized Glacier National Park, an amazingly beautiful preserve in the Rockies of Northern Montana.

The idea of preserving the landscape of America for future generations had come a long way. But with all that land set aside for public use, no one had come up with a cohesive plan to make sure it was used correctly.

President Taft was one of the first to call for action in that direction. Though all the areas designated as Parks and Monuments were under the control of the Interior Department, each had its own rules, many of which didn't work. Taft asked Congress to help him do something about it. "The department is the 'lumber room' of the Government," he told them "into which we put everything we don't know how to classify."

That was in 1911. In 1916, Congress finally gave the Department of the Interior a separate division to run the Parks. A tiny budget was appropriated and an idea that had been kicking around for 44 years and had often come close to being kicked to death was given a new lease of life.

To say that the idea of preserving the landscape of America by legislation is one that has stood the test of time would be a mild form of hubris. The real legislation is less than 75 years old, after all, and there are still assaults being made on it. But though the protected landscape is only a small part of our natural heritage, it is an important one and anyone who owns a car has a good idea of what might have been if the Parks System hadn't been created.

A Texan who once described the territory surrounding his home town as "so beautiful it hurts your eyes", spends most Sunday afternoons going up and down the nearby hills on a dirt bike; a noisy little motorcycle that kicks up a lot of dust and leaves deep tracks in its wake. Up in Vermont, where the snow-filled winter woods are so quiet you can almost hear the silence, the noise you do hear is made by the snowmobiles; vehicles that have given a new meaning to the term "joyriding".

In a New York suburb, the owner of a small factory whose waste has killed most of the vegetation along a Pennsylvania creek spends $30,000 a year to keep the grounds of his fenced-in estate trimmed, clipped and forever green. In California, a group of young people who have organized a continuing demonstration against the construction of a nuclear power plant create nearly as much litter on the site as the debris piled up in the construction process.

Every one of those people is law-abiding, civic-minded, sensitive. They all support the idea that the landscape ought to be preserved for their children and grand-children. And many give more than just lip service to such ideals.

But destruction of the landscape isn't always a wanton act. It isn't always avoidable.

A poet sees a snow-covered mountain as a perfect place for quiet reflection. But it also can be a great place to ski. The folks who live in a tiny Iowa crossroads town weren't too pleased to have an Interstate highway built less than a mile from their front porches, but they haven't had trucks roaring through town in the middle of the night ever since it was finished. It's what we like to call "progress". It's what we've long-since come to regard as inevitable.

In a manner of speaking, we have, in fact, progressed a great deal. People have begun to care.

From Colonial times there was plenty of land for everyone out there, and not many people to fill it. Even Thomas Jefferson, who would never be accused of being insensitive to man or nature, couldn't help saying: "Utility to man is the standard and test of virtue". When Americans began moving West in the early 19th century, they cleared huge farms and then proceeded to work them to death. When the land wasn't productive any longer, they just moved further West. Life may have been hard, but it was simple. In Oklahoma and Texas in the early 20th century they covered the plains with wheat farms that eventually dried up and blew away. "Progress" came in the form of reclaiming what they had destroyed.

The romantic vision of our immediate ancestors is of hard-working men and women who respected nature and learned to live in harmony with it. A more realistic picture is often of people who learned to live in spite of it.

There is probably not a mountain range in the world more beautiful than the Rockies. But people following the cause of Horace Greeley's Manifest Destiny must have wondered, when they saw them rising up out across the plains, whether God hadn't played some cruel joke when He placed them there. Many never made it across. Some who trekked west by the northern route never ventured past the Black Hills of South Dakota, and a place they always gave a wide berth to was the territory east of there which they called "hell with the fires out"; known to this day as The Badlands.

In many parts of America you can tell what the terrain is like simply by looking at names on a map. Pleasant Hills, Pennsylvania invites you to linger a while. Cape Fear in Virginia might be a place you'd want to steer around. There are Bald Mountains and Lovers' Leaps in just about every state, even though the former may be tree-covered by now and the latter probably never was the site of a romantic suicide.

Naming the place was the fun part for every party of early explorers and discoverers. When the Vikings came, if indeed they ever really did, they didn't bring a whole lot of imagination and the places they noted on their charts were called such things as Vineland and Woodland. The Spanish and Portuguese added a flair by rarely naming a place without an all-day ceremony that included the erection of a cross, a high mass and a little cannon-firing to impress the natives. They often named places after the Royal patrons they had left behind, but still wanted to impress. Possibly even more often, the name came from the saint on whose day the place was discovered; a much more important person to impress, to be sure.

When the English began settling New England, they were more liberal in keeping the old Indian names, but to show they, too, were God-fearing people, they turned to the Bible for such names as Salem and Lebanon. In contrast to the Spanish, they scrupulously avoided the saints. As their historian, Cotton Mather, explained, "We have but one protector in heaven, and that is our Lord Jesus Christ". But let the record show that in spite of that statement there is no such place in New England as "East Jesus"; a popular cliche used to describe any out-of-the-way place.

New Englanders were the first Americans to make wholesale use of the names of towns they had left behind. The official reason was to perpetuate a memory of a former life they missed. The real reason was that they knew their only real hope for survival and a prosperous future was to lure new colonists to this side of the Atlantic. They knew that such names as Scituate and Acushnet suggested to English ears that this was probably a wild, savage place so they civilized it with names like Exeter, Hartford and Windsor.

The Virginians, who never quite cut the cord with English Royalty, respectfully named the first river they found after King James and established colonies near Williamsburg and Charlottesville.

Not all the words they brought with them from England quite suited the landscape of America. Where the Old Country had running brooks, their new home seemed to have roaring creeks. America didn't offer much in the way of heaths, either, so another venerable English word was conspicuous by its absence on American maps. Where England had bogs, America has swamps; where they had ponds, we had small lakes, but the name pond fitted comfortably enough. Up in New England, for lack of a better term, they called gaps in the mountains "notches". Later when the country moved west and the mountains got bigger, so did the gaps and another word was needed. "Passes" passed muster. The early settlers hadn't had much experience with mountains that rose abruptly above their neighbors. In the East they were content to call them "knobs", but got more grandiose about it before the westward trek began. The passion for Biblical names changed knobs overnight to such things as Mount Zion or Mount Sinai and in the process began a new American tradition of naming the high peaks "Mount" while often dropping the word "mountain" from the names of such ranges as the Sierra Nevada or the Appalachians.

The French mapmakers and explorers added their own touches to the names of the landscape. They shared the Spanish passion for honoring saints and the English enthusiasm for currying Royal favour. But they weren't above naming rivers and streams and other natural features after themselves. And why not? If you're going to impress someone, picking future generations isn't a bad idea. After the Sieur de Champlain tangled with some Indians on a lake shore in 1609, he wrote in his report of the battle that it had taken place on a lake known as Lake Champlain. It hadn't been until then, but it is now.

There is no such thing as a professional place-namer. Anybody who knows the difference between a river and a creek, a waterfall and rapids can play the game. But when Europeans first began arriving in North America, there were features on the landscape that needed to be studied, and named, by professionals. The plant life they found was not only different from that back home, but some of the trees apparently had properties the people back home would pay good prices for. One of the first they noticed in the Virginia Colony was the sassafras tree. The Indians used its bark to

cure fevers. The English thought that, all by itself, would make the tree a good cash crop. The importers must have had a very good PR man on their payroll because not long after the first shiploads of sassafras bark began arriving in England, curing fevers was only one reason for buying it. Another was that it seemed to keep the bugs away. Some said it could make broken bones knit faster. Others said it could cure baldness. Everyone knew for sure it was an elixir of youth. But the thing that kept demand ahead of supply was the conviction that the Virginia Colony had produced the world's first cure for syphilis.

It wasn't true, of course, but it sold a lot of sassafras. Virginians were also doing a good business at the time exporting the leaves of another plant called tobacco. The first dried leaves were taken to England by Sir Walter Raleigh who said that the Indians inhaled the smoke produced by burning them and "by this means keep in excellent health". He told his future customers that the smoke "preserves the body, and if there are any obstructions, it breaks them up". Of course, by the time anyone had experimented enough to find out that was a lot of nonsense, they already had the habit.

Botany was a brand-new science in those days, but there was probably not a spot on earth more alluring to the men who practiced it than this newly-developing continent. And it was good business to encourage them.

Oddly, they got no formal encouragement until 1748 when the Swedish Government sent botanist Peter Kalm to Philadelphia to scout around to see if any American trees or plants might thrive in Sweden. On his travels north through the Hudson Valley and up to Quebec, he discovered more than 60 new plants and found out that it's true what they say about poison ivy. He also discovered the love of his life in New Jersey, married her and took her home with him.

What he left behind is a plant he is credited with finding and classifying, the state flower of Pennsylvania; the mountain laurel. The route he took to the north still abounds in it, which is why it's such a wonderful place to be in the late spring.

By the beginning of the 19th century, most of the East Coast had been explored and its plant life recorded by these adventuresome scientists. But the first to cross the country completely was Thomas Nuttall, who made several trips, beginning in 1809, including an adventure with John Jacob Astor's fur trappers who followed the Lewis and Clark expedition into Oregon. He only made it as far as central North Dakota on that occasion, but in the process explored and classified trees and plants along the entire length of the Mississippi and most of the Missouri River. Later, he was the first to take such a trip along most of the length of the Arkansas River. He finally made it to the Columbia River and the Pacific Northwest in 1834 and, just for the fun of it, took a side trip to Hawaii when the expedition was over.

Nuttall wasn't the first botanist to collect specimens in the Pacific Northwest. A 1792 expedition under the command of Captain George Vancouver had included a botanist who described some of the plants he found there, including giant evergreens the like of which no Englishman had ever seen before. Thirty-two years later, but still a decade ahead of Nuttall, David Douglas was to share that experience, lending his name to the magnificent fir trees that he encountered along the Columbia River.

He got there the same way Vancouver did, by ship from England. He had been to America before on an earlier mission similar to the journeys of Peter Kalm on behalf of the Swedish Government. Douglas was asked to explore the East Coast as far north and west as Detroit looking for plants and trees that could be grown in England. During his first trip he had seen New York and the Hudson River, he had seen the Great Lakes and Niagara Falls, but he had never seen anything quite like the Pacific Northwest. In 1824, not many white men had seen it at all. David Douglas hadn't seen anything yet.

The ship that had brought him was continuing north and would be back through in six months. Douglas was determined to collect as many new specimens as possible to have on board when the ship sailed back. By the time it did, he had collected nearly 500 on a trip that had taken him deep inland along the Columbia River. It wasn't an easy job. To begin with, it rains a lot along the Columbia River, which is one of the reasons the moss is often six inches thick. But botanical specimens need to be dried or they die and become useless for study. And even though a botanist is forced to become a slow walker, it's tiring work, and sleeping with a wet blanket has never been satisfying. Once past the mountains it rains very little, which is terrific for drying plants, but it gets hot and the bright sun is hard on the eyes. But if any of those things bothered David Douglas, he didn't say so.

He was travelling alone in Indian country and his search for new plants took his attention away from cautiously watching for danger. But he was good with a rifle and it was the first thing the watchful Indians noticed about him. That earned him their respect, but they still thought he was a little odd and smirkingly called him "Grassman" because of his strange preoccupation with plants and his even stranger excitement when he found a new one. But if he was a little funny in the head, he seemed harmless to them, even though his rifle gave him a bit of an edge.

Left alone he was able to revel in the unbelievable beauty of the place. And when he wasn't searching the ground for new wildflowers, he was looking up in awe at the endless variety of evergreens that grew there. Though he himself didn't name the Douglas Fir, it was among the varieties that he admired most. It was on this trip he was able to measure one for the first time and found, to his amazement, that it was almost 230 feet high. It was also during his first six months in this wonderland that he identified the Western white pine, the ponderosa pine, the silver fir and dozens of other varieties.

But then he made a discovery that made all others seem puny.

The Indians were not only not hostile to him, but many actually befriended him and one day one of them offered to share some nuts with him. But they weren't nuts, they were pine seeds, obviously from a cone much bigger than anything Douglas had ever imagined. He asked the Indian where they came from and was told they grew far away in the south.

That, in a nutshell as it were, is why David Douglas turned south.

The Indians warned him of evil spirits. Trappers warned him of endless rain. He hadn't gone far when he saw evidence of grizzly bears. But it was worth enduring anything to find the tree that produced those pinecones. Exactly 35 days later, after nearly being killed in a fall, after encounters with hostile Indians, after more continuous days of rain than he had ever seen in England, David Douglas found his tree in the middle of Oregon. Few men have experienced such joy.

The tree he found was well over 200 feet high, the trunk measured 57 feet around. And there on the lowest branch, 100 feet above his head, were some of the biggest pinecones God ever made; some more than two feet long. But there was a problem. There was no way to get at them, and a botanist without samples is little more than a sightseer. He made sketches of the wonderous cones, but he hadn't come this far to go back empty-handed.

His solution was to use his pistol to shoot one down and his aim was good enough that he did it with a single shot. But this was enough to attract the attention of an Indian hunting party, none of whom seemed to find him as quaint as their neighbors up north had. Douglas tried smiling and seeming friendly but that didn't work at all. The angry stares intensified. So he did what you'd expect a mild-mannered botanist to do. He aimed his rifle at the leader's chest and waved his pistol in the general direction of the other six. And stopped smiling. They finally backed off and began smiling themselves and then told Douglas they'd let him go if he gave them some tobacco. But David Douglas was born in Scotland. He wanted more for his money. He told them he'd give them the tobacco if they'd get him more of those giant pinecones to take with him when they let him go. It must have been the glint in his eye that convinced them because they gathered more than he could carry.

The tree he found was the Western sugar pine, far and away the biggest member of its family. The discovery was the high point of his career but it was far from the end of it.

He carried the cones back to the mouth of the Columbia where he packed them with other specimens to be sent back to England and then set off on the last leg of his adventure; a trip across Canada, collecting specimens all the way of course, to an outpost on Hudson's Bay where he could catch a ship that would take him home.

By the time he got there, two shipments he had sent on ahead had made him a very famous young man. But he hadn't walked all that distance just to achieve fame, and before long he was on his way back to America on a trip that would take him north into Alaska and south to California. As Thomas Nuttall would a year later, he decided to go home this time by way of Hawaii. It represented a new landscape to conquer. It would conquer him.

On the day he intended to leave, he went for a walk in the mountains and slipped into a pit that had been dug to trap wild bulls. Unfortunately, a bull had already fallen into the trap. David Douglas was only 35 years old when he died, but in that short time he had collected more varieties of trees and flowers, a great many of which were cultivated and are contributing to the beauty of the man-made American landscape today, than any man before him.

The landscape of America, both natural and man-made, is as unique as it is indescribable. Almost every kind of food crop, from oranges to winter wheat, is grown on its farms and orchards. It is a land of rugged, awe-inspiring mountains and forested gentle ridges. Its sea coasts are composed of rocky cliffs and sandy beaches. Its climate ranges from almost eternal sunshine to summers that seem to pass in the twinkling of an eye. There are tropical rainforests in its boundaries and areas so barren they seem to belong to another world. Flatlands range inland almost as far as the eye can see from much of the Atlantic shore while the Pacific dashes furiously on high, rocky palisades. America is a land that has alternately been covered by oceans and glaciers. It has experienced the violence of earthquakes and volcanoes. All of them have left their marks on the landscape.

The hardwood forests of the Southeast and the softwood

forests of the Northwest are places where rhododendrons thrive, and yet the two areas are unmistakably different. The vineyards of California and the cranberry bogs of Cape Cod have nothing at all in common, yet the landscape of America easily accommodates both.

Yet for all that, if you were suddenly dropped into the suburbs of Houston or Miami or Los Angeles the landscape would be remarkably similar. Only the rise and fall of the land is different. The gas stations and fast food stands are the same everywhere, and the houses vary little from region to region except in price. Motels are made to look alike to make travellers feel at home. Shopping centers, always trying to distinguish themselves from each other, never seem to escape a standard mold.

Our ancestors were proud of regional differences, but all that remains of anything that makes one section of America different from another is what there was all along; the landscape itself.

Back in the days when oil companies were beginning to talk about building a pipeline to get oil down from the North Slope of Alaska, many Americans got their first peek at the vast tundra there via television from, of all people, the comic philosopher Jean Shepard.

He had a program on public television then, in which he made it a point to show us what we really looked like. His segment on Alaska ended as he marched endless yards across the tundra, getting further and further away from a stationary camera, all the while talking about what an unusual, untouched place this is. Then, as his figure became almost nothing more than a dot on the horizon, he suddenly stopped. "I've found something", he shouted, "out where no man has ever been! . . . Look at this! . . . A rusty beer can!".

The hand of man had struck again.

On the other hand, back in 1863, Mark Twain said of the American countryside:

"As a dwelling place for civilized man, it is by far the first upon our globe".

Trunk Bay *facing page,* with its round-contoured islands
and soft, golden beaches washed by the lapping waters of
the Caribbean, is typical of the enticing Virgin Islands
scenery. *Above:* the warm light of evening descends on a
peaceful Maho Bay.

Located in the Chugach National Forest, not far from the
city of Anchorage, stands the majestic Portage Glacier
these pages, its sparkling, candy-like surface reflecting the
vivid blue color of a clear, freezing sky.

The golden light of a spectacular sunset near Valdez,
Alaska, breathes life into the thickening, boulder-strewn
waters of Mineral Creek *facing page*, contrasting with the
tilled-looking field of steaming ice on Turnagain Arm *below*.

9

Milolii, at the southern end of the island of Hawaii, is a tiny Hawaiian-Filipino fishing community. The land consists mainly of lava rubble *above* supporting palms and a few other plants. Devastation Trail *right* is half a mile of boardwalk ending at Kilauea Iki Overlook and Puu Puai, a huge cone of ash and pumice resulting from a 1959 eruption.

12

Heavy and low-lying storm clouds almost obscure Oahu's Koolau Range, seen from Laie Point *left* **and the Pali coast, on the island of Molokai** *above.*

The glorious reds and golds of a Hawaiian sunset
silhouette the palm trees and St. Peter's Catholic Church
above as well as people out for an evening stroll or swim at
Ala Moana Park, Oahu, Honolulu, *facing page.*

Like a scene from Dante's 'Inferno' steam rises menacingly *above* from Halemaumau Firepit, in Hawaii's Kilauea Crater. Tufts of grass dot the contorted landscape *right* of a typical lava field on the west coast of Hawaii.

Above: **the Silversword** *(Argyroxiphium sandwicense)* **is a**
dramatic and unusual annual to be found only on the
islands. Cattle *facing page* **peacefully graze the pastures of**
the Parker Ranch, reputedly the largest – some 200,000
acres – private ranch in the U.S.A.

Almost defoliated trees, their texture enhanced by the late evening sun, at Waimea Canyon *above,* **and a typical Hawaiian sunset at Kahului Bay** *facing page* **on Maui Island.**

The twin tunnels of the highway on Oahu Island cut right
through the Koolau Range *facing page*. The eroded
landscape of Waimea Canyon *above* is pictured from 3,400

Dense vegetation in the Nuuana Valley Rain Forest *above*
on the island of Oahu. *Facing page:* **a calm sunset on the**
west coast of Maui.

The incredibly blue Crater Lake, Oregon *these pages,* **is something of a mystery. There is no inlet and outlet of water; no waterfalls fill it and no streams drain it, yet the snow and rain are in perfect balance with evaporation. There has been only the slightest variation in the total volume through the years it has been measured. Many volcanic crater lakes exist in the world, but none quite like this.**

Above: **Bench Lake, in Washington State. Rising from the blue waters of Crater Lake** *right* **is the symmetrical cinder cone of Wizard Island.**

The brilliant gold of the setting sun's pathway reaches
across the waters of Great Bend, on the Hood Canal,
Washington State *above* and a lone fishing boat *facing page*
waits on Fish Lake in the eerie half-light of gathering dusk.

Sculpted by the elements, the remains of a once mighty
tree *above* lies on Rialto Beach, in the scenic wilderness of
Olympic National Park, where the boat *facing page* skims
across the sunlit surface of the Hood Canal.

The peaks of the Olympic Range turn to varying shades of
blue and purple in the twilight across Great Bend, on the
Hood Canal *left.* Dwarfed by the massive landscape

Like an abstract painting *above* or a carelessly-thrown green blanket *facing page* the fertile acres of Palouse Farming Country, Bitter Root Mountains, stretch as far as the eye can see.

Extending across Washington State from north to south, paralleling the Columbia River, is the Cascade mountain range *above*. The late sun illuminates the face of Mount Chuksan *facing page* as clouds drift below the summit.

From the air, Washington State's Cascade Mountains, in common with all other mountain ranges, take on a different aspect. The enormous upheavals that created them are even more cause for wonder, and the jagged ridges and peaks stand out sharply against the blue of the sky and the white snow. *Facing page:* the massive bulk of Glacier Peak stands in proud isolation on the horizon.

The golden landscape of endless wheat fields in Palouse farming country *above. Right:* **Mount Adams, in the southern part of Washington State.**

Between the blue of the flowers and the deeper blue of the sky, Mount Rainier, in Mount Rainier National Park, *left* rises to a height of 14,410 feet. *Above:* Diablo Lake with Mount Challenger in the background.

Overleaf: generations of large-scale wheat growers have contributed to the manicured look of mile upon mile of the rich Palouse farmland *left.* Shown *right* is Picture Lake in the Northern Cascades.

Picturesque in the mist, but perilous for shipping, Cape Disappointment Lighthouse *above* **marks the mouth of the Columbia River. The Olympic Rain Forest** *facing page,* **a luxuriant green woodland, rivals any tropical rain forest for beauty and wildlife.**

Below: **Blue mist in Lady Bird Johnson Grove, Redwood National Park, California.** *Facing page:* **coastal fog over redwoods at sunset, California.**

51

Sky and sea meet in studies in blue and gold on the rock-strewn coast at Point St. George, California, *these pages.*

Above: the marvelously folded landscape, the rocky coastline and Cabrillo Highway on the California coast south of Carmel. *Left:* Bixby Creek Bridge, Monterey.

55

Over the centuries the incessant pounding of the waves, together with the wind and the rain, have formed the fascinating coastline at Point Lobos *above* and Gray Whale Cove, north of Montara, California *right*.

Seen from the air are the magnificent coastal settings of
California's Cypress Point golf course *facing page* and the
sixth and seventh holes of Pebble Beach golf course *above*.

63

In isolated splendor Lassen Peak *above* rises beyond snow
and ice-encrusted Lake Helen. Seething mud pots, hissing
hot springs and barren, volcanic landscapes: Bumpass Hell
right in Lassen Volcanic National Park, California.

In the fascinating and remarkable Lassen Volcanic
National Park, Hat Creek *above* rushes between its green
banks, and a few trees manage to find a foothold in the
fantastic lava beds known as the 'Painted Dunes' *facing
page.*

Snow lies thick on the ground and bends the branches of
the trees bordering California's Lake Tahoe *facing page*. A
bubbling mud pool *above* in Lassen Volcanic National
Park's Bumpass Hell.

Above: **Upper Yosemite Valley seen from Glacier Point, in Yosemite National Park. Also in the park, pictured from Washburn Point, Nevada (upper) and Vernal (lower) Falls appear diminutive as the river threads its way through the towering landscape** *facing page.*

71

Sequoia National Park, California. *Facing page:* Columbine Lake and Lost Canyon and *above:* Monarch Lakes, Rainbow Mountain and Mineral Peak.

Trees survive where once the glacier carved Tenaya
Canyon *facing page*, in Yosemite. In contrast is the still
beauty of Mirror Lake and Mount Watkins *above*.

The awesome grandeur of Yosemite. *Above:* **Kings Canyon**
and *right* **Bridalveil Falls at the end of Yosemite Valley.**

The heart of California's wine country lies in the Napa Valley *above. Facing page:* **in the rich colors of fall, the cowboy and his horse create exactly the right mood in this**

At Death Valley National Monument in California lies the
aptly-named Devil's Golfcourse *left*, part of the valley
floor's immense sea of salt, and Ubehebe Crater *above*, a
result of volcanic activity.

A softer echo of the ridges beyond them, sand dunes *facing page* in Death Valley. *Above:* Artist's Palette, also to be found in the varied scenery of Death Valley National

Two views of the torn and faulted landscape of Death Valley: Golden Canyon *above* **and the scene that meets the eye from Zabriskie Point** *facing page.*

Above: the lonely expanse of the Anza-Borrego Desert
State Park, San Diego County, California. Varied flora
facing page in the Living Desert Reserve, Palm Desert, near
Palm Springs.

Left: **the Palm Springs Tramway, in Riverside County, California.** *Below:* **a mere speck in the convoluted landscape of Palm Springs: Bob Hope's house from the air.**

Brooding in the distance, Superstition Mountains *above* take their name from the legends handed down in which they feature. Fields of alfalfa *facing page* are watered by the essential irrigation system provided by a series of dams throughout Arizona.

Arizona's Petrified Forest is unique among the
petrifications of the world in its size, variety and scope.
Facing page: logs turned to stone over the ages lie scattered
in Blue Mesa. *Above:* Painted Desert – a strange landscape
of weird shapes and marvelous variety of color.

In Grand Canyon, layer upon layer of stratified rock rises from the canyon floor, where the Colorado River, seen at Lee's Ferry *above*, winds like a slender ribbon. Reflecting the sun's warm rays stands the brilliantly-colored rock formation of Cathedral Rock *facing page* at Red Rock Crossing in Sedona's Oak Creek Canyon.

Sunsets produce their own brand of magic in these scenes
facing page **of the San Francisco Peaks near Flagstaff and
the giant Saguaro cactus in Desert Foothills, Phoenix,
Arizona** *above.*

Arizona's scenery and monuments rank among the most
magnificent in the country. Oak Creek Canyon is shown
above while *facing page* is pictured majestic Monument
Valley.

Different moods *above and left,* **but equally awe-inspiring:
East and West Mittens, with Merrick Butte, in Monument
Valley's Navajo Trail Park.**

Wherever the eye rests there is something new to be seen of the ancient and incredible landscapes of the Grand Canyon *facing page* and the Petrified Forest National Park *above*.

From the majestic peaks of Hopi Point *above and facing page* the splendor of the Grand Canyon's South Rim fans out to meet the horizon.

The Grand Canyon has often been described as a sight too staggering, too vast for the imagination to take in. *Facing page:* the view from Moran Point and *above* from Yaki Point.

At times, depending on the light and the weather, the
Grand Canyon can appear forbidding, frightening almost;
at other times, as here in the views from Mohave Point
above and Yaki Point *facing page,* there is an aura of peace;
a mystic stillness.

Canyon de Chelly *left* in Arizona, contains evidence of five
different periods of Indian culture. *Above:* Little Colorado
River Gorge, near Gray Mountain.

Formed in a limestone reef by percolating ground water, the vast underground chambers of the Carlsbad Caverns *above and facing page* are situated beneath the rugged foothills of New Mexico's Guadaloupe Mountains. In this subterranean wonderland the huge galleries are filled with delicate stone formations, massive stalactites and stalagmites which, colored by the minerals and iron they contain, produce a fascinating, iridescent glow.

Silhouetted by the late evening sun, a lone tree *above* in New Mexico's Gila National Forest. *Facing page:* the sun breaks through the clouds above the Sangre de Cristo Mountains, New Mexico.

The Saguaro National Monument *facing page* **contains dense stands of Saguaro cactus which can live up to 200 years, reaching heights of 36 feet and, exceptionally, 50 feet. Aloof and gaunt, the massive bulk of Shiprock** *below* **is seen sharply outlined against a glowing sunset.**

Left: **the undulating dunes of the Monahans Sandhills, Texas.** *Above:* **covering almost 300 square miles, the dazzling white gypsum sands of New Mexico's White Sands National Monument shimmer like an alabaster sea.**

Among the commoner plants in the Guadaloupe National Park is the spiky, smooth-leafed sotol *facing page,* pictured with Hunter Peak in the background. *Above:* Inscription Rock at El Morro National Monument, New Mexico.

125

127

Zion Canyon, in Zion National Park, Utah, is a spectacular
multicolored gorge, where gigantic stone masses such as
the Watchman *left* and the Sentinel *above,* may be seen
across the waters of the North Fork of the Virgin River.

The colorful and quite incredible formations in Bryce Canyon are the result of rocks, shale and sandstones which have all eroded at different rates, allowing the elements to create fantastic sculptures and free-standing columns *above*. The last of the sun just catches one of the peaks at

Heavy clouds gathering at Bryce Canyon's Paria View
above. **One of the remarkable scenes** *facing page* **on the**
Fairyland Trail, Bryce Canyon, Utah.

133

134

Left: **Bryce Point, Bryce Canyon National Park.** *Above:* **an ink-black sky adds drama – if that were possible – to the pinnacles, spires and slopes seen from Inspiration Point.**

In Canyonlands National Park, Utah, the sun silhouettes
both tiny figures and massive rock formations *above,* seen
from Big Spring Canyon Overlook. Arches National Park
lies in the famous red rock country of Utah and contains
more natural stone arches – such as Delicate Arch *facing
page* – windows, spires and pinnacles than anywhere else
in the country.

Against the huge ball of the setting sun, trucks *above* cross
a bridge near Las Cruces, Colorado, and *facing page* an
electric storm demonstrates its power above the state's
Mesa Verde National Park.

Horses grazing *above* **against the backdrop of a Colorado forest.** *Facing page:* **Dream Lake with Hallett Peak and Flattop Mountain in the background.**

The gold of autumn leaves decorates a tree *facing page* overlooking Bear Lake in Rocky Mountain National Park, Colorado, and a whole lakeside is turned to yellows and golds *above* near Colorado's Pyramid Peak.

Each season has its own especial beauty, but the magic of fall has, for most people, an irresistible charm, as here in Colorado's Crystal Creek *above* **and Independence Pass** *facing page.*

A late-summer sky reflected in the still waters of the Blue
Mesa Reservoir *above* in the Curecanti National Recreation
Area, and *facing page* in the scene at Shallow Creek Lane,
near Creede, Colorado.

Spread like a vast green and gold sea, the hills around
Ashcroft, near Aspen, flood the landscape *above* with their
vibrant colors. *Facing page:* the tranquil scene at Beaver
Ponds, in Hidden Valley, Colorado.

The wide, rolling plains of Gunnison County *left* with, in
the background, thickly-forested, undulating hills rising to
meet a darkening sky. Huge sand dunes *above* separate the
tree-filled foreground from the towering bulk of the Sangre
de Cristo Mountains in Colorado.

The swirling waters of the Cimarron River *facing page*
shown bordered by russet-leaved trees. Beyond the
shadowed lake and trees, within the majestic San Juan
Range, is Red Mountain *above*

Sculpted by glaciers during the Ice Age, the serrated peaks of the Grand Tetons, as they rise abruptly from the valley floor, form a magnificent backdrop for the autumnal-hued trees *above.* **The peaks of the Grand Teton Range rise beyond the waters of the Snake River at Oxbow Bend** *facing page.*

Sunset at Jackson Lake *above*, set among the Grand Teton
Mountains. The Morning Glory Pool *facing page* in
Yellowstone National Park, Wyoming, was so named
because of the resemblance of its bowl and color to the
corolla and color of the morning glory flower.

159

Minerva Terrace *above*, **Mammoth Hot Springs,**
Yellowstone National Park, is composed of travertine, a

Lower Green Lake and Flattop Mountain *above*. **Burnished at sunset, Wyoming's Jackson Lake** *facing page* **is a natural lake formed in a deep groove left by a piedmont glacier which passed through Jackson Hole during the first Ice Age.**

The Lower Falls of the Yellowstone River *above*. **The waters
of the river fall a breathtaking 308 feet at this point, while
at the Upper Falls** *facing page* **the torrent arches gracefully
out and down for 109 feet.**

Morning Glory
Pool

Bison *facing page* **at the aptly-named Opalescent Pool,**
which brings ever changing shades to Black Sand Basin.
Above: **Yellowstone's Morning Glory Pool, complete with**

Producing clouds of steam, even in the cold of winter,
Midway Geyser Basin, Wyoming, is pictured *above* **while**
bison graze during a dull winter's day at Black Sand Basin

Fire-Ball River, colored as befits its name *facing page*
curves through Wyoming's Midway Geyser. Part of the
natural beauty which makes Yellowstone so idyllic a
preserve, the Gibbon River *below* threads its silver waters
between the trees and grassland of its banks

Horses *above* **forage for sparse sustenance in the bleak winter landscape near Laramie, Wyoming.** *Facing page:* **a heavily clouded sky above flooded grassland in Montana.**

Sunrise goldens Mount Sinopah beyond the shores of Two Medicine Lake *above* **and jagged mountains surround St. Mary Lake and Wild Geese Island** *facing page*, **in Glacier National Park, Montana.**

The Wild West lives again in the scenes *above and facing page* **during Monterey's annual bison round-up.**

The Badlands National Monument *these pages* **lies in southwestern South Dakota. It was established in 1939 in the area between the Cheyenne and White Rivers. The monument contains numerous fossil beds in which has been found evidence of such exotic animals as the sabre-toothed tiger and the rhinoceros.**

The Mississippi River *above;* that mighty river that reaches to the Gulf of Mexico, has its source in Minnesota's Lake Itasca. *Facing page:* Upper Herring Lake, near Frankfort, Northwest Michigan.

A golden, contemplative sunset *above* at Presque Isle
Point, Lake Superior, near Marquette, Upper Peninsula,
Michigan. Equally mind-soothing, the rushing waters of
Lower Tahquamenon Falls, Michigan *facing page*.

Evening descends *facing page* **over the softly-rippling surface of Traverse Bay, Lake Michigan, while** *above* **is seen the graceful Mackinac Bridge, which connects Michigan's Upper and Lower peninsulas.**

Proudly displaying its name atop one of its huge
supporting structures is the graceful Ambassador Bridge
facing page, spanning the Detroit River.

Farms, and acres of arable farmland dot the fertile
countryside of the varied state of Wisconsin. *Above* is
shown a farm building typical of the area.

The huge golden orb of the setting sun hangs in a fiery
red sky over La Crosse, Wisconsin *above* while in complete
contrast is the shadowed walkway in Wisconsin Dells *facing
page.*

Over the years, people have largely moved off the land in
Ohio, abandoning farms for work in the factories. Plenty of
farms still remain, however, such as that *above* at Somerset,
and Bob Even's farm at Rio Grande *facing page*.

Industry old and new in Ohio. *Above* is Indian Mill,
overlooking the Sandusky River, in Wyandot County and,
facing page, the huge complex of the United States Steel
Mill in Cleveland.

Along the waterfront of St. Louis riverboats such as the
Robert E. Lee *facing page* still ply the waters of the
Mississippi. Symbolic of St. Louis, Eero Saarinen's awe-
inspiring stainless steel 'Gateway Arch' is shown *above*
silhouetted against the orange sunset.

Fall colors glow softly in the evening sun at Cades Cove
above, **and** *facing page* **is shown Little River, both in the
Great Smoky Mountains National Park, Tennessee.**

In Great Smoky Mountains National Park, mist hangs between the tree-covered mountain slopes *above*, seen from Newfound Gap Road. *Facing page:* overhung with trees, Little Pigeon River rushes its way along its boulder-strewn bed.

Kentucky is renowned for its fine thoroughbred horses
above **which grow sleek on the rich pasture of the**
Bluegrass. Nine original slave houses, lining the 'Avenue of
the Oaks' have been preserved *facing page* **on the Boone**
Hill Plantation, Charleston, South Carolina.

In South Carolina, slave houses *above* on the Boone Hill
Plantation contrast tellingly with the splendour of
beautiful Drayton Hall *facing page*.

Almost the first thing that comes to mind when 'Louisiana'
is mentioned is 'Mississippi'. The mighty river is shown
above as it sweeps past the famed city of New Orleans and
facing page is the river boat "Natchez" with the
Mississippi Bridge in the background.

Sunset over the calm waters of Florida's Key West *above*
and in the Everglades National Park *facing page.*

217

Facing page: **moss-festooned trees silhouetted in a Florida sunset.** *Above:* **the Swannee River in northern Florida.**

Fifty years ago Miami Beach *facing page and above* was a wilderness of mangrove swamps, infested with snakes and mosquitoes. Today it is the largest resort in the world, attracting visitors from many countries eager to enjoy the luxury hotels, subtropical climate and fine beaches.

Florida's spectacular peninsula separates the Atlantic
Ocean and the Florida Straits from the blue waters of the
Gulf of Mexico. The picture *facing page* shows a scene in
the remarkable Cypress Mangrove Swamp in the Everglades
National Park, and *above* is the Caloosahatchee River
Bridge at Fort Myers.

Fishing is a much-favored occupation and recreation at Key West *facing page*, where fishing boats are shown at anchor at sunset.

Above is the Kingsley Plantation House, Fort George Island, Florida.

The same fine weather that brings vacationers flocking to sundrenched Florida can cause problems for farmers, hence the use of the 'water cannons' in the fields near South Miami *above*. A glorious sunset *facing page* is reflected in the water at Florida's Tarpon Springs.

Many fine and historic houses have been restored *above* **in Williamsburg, Virginia, to recreate and preserve the atmosphere of its 18th-century existence.**
Facing page: **a wintry scene at Norfolk, Virginia.**

Colonial Williamsburg *these pages,* carefully restored to
capture the atmosphere and appearance of its 18th century
existence, was the capital of Virginia between 1699 and
1799. The aim of the preservation project, begun in 1926 and
administered by the Colonial Williamsburg Foundation, was
to recreate as faithfully as possible this colorful
period of American history.

A thin blanket of snow covers the winter landscape of New
Market Battlefield Park in Virginia's Shenandoah Valley
above and facing page.

In an idyllic setting, as though untouched by time, stands
Mabry Mill *left,* along the Blue Ridge Parkway.
   Cattle *above* graze the meadows of Dan Farm, also on
Virginia's Blue Ridge Parkway.

Its new timbers starkly contrasted against the snow, the
covered bridge *above* lies in the Shenandoah Valley.
  Facing page is pictured a farm near Rose Hill, in
Virginia.

The richness of fall's coloring adds another dimension to the beauty of the scenes *above and facing page* **of a farm nestled in the Ground Hog Mountain landscape of the Blue Ridge Parkway.**

The famed Shenandoah River *above and facing page* at
Harper's Ferry, in the Blue Ridge Mountains, where West
Virginia, Virginia and Maryland converge. The site was
selected by George Washington for a federal armory because
of its water-power potential and it was purchased from
Harper's heirs in 1796.

The railroad bridge *above and facing page* at Harper's Ferry. It was at Harper's Ferry, in 1859, that John Brown launched his anti-slavery raid against the County Militia and Citizen Volunteers in a bid to capture the arsenal and armory.

Most of the summer's harvest now safely gathered, two
isolated farms *above and facing page* nestle at the foot of
Maryland's Appalachian mountain range.

A barge *above* laboriously negotiates a series of locks in
the Chesapeake and Ohio canal, which runs through the
Georgetown area of Washington D.C. The monolithic
Washington Monument *facing page* soars above the trees at
the Mall's western end.

The annual blooming of the Japanese cherry blossom marks
the unofficial start of spring in the capital, Washington
D.C. Each year thousands of visitors flock to the city to
enjoy the spectacle. Framed by the blossom are the
soaring Washington Monument *facing page* and the beautiful
Jefferson Memorial *above.*

South of Savannah, Georgia, on one of the 'Golden Isles' –
St. Simon's Island – stands Christ Church, Frederica
facing page, built where the Wesley brothers preached to
the first congregation in Oglethorpe's settlement. Jekyll
Island, once a favorite haunt of millionaires, has many
houses such as the lovely example *above.*

Philadelphia's Benjamin Franklin Bridge *facing page* crosses the
Delaware River from the city center to Camden.
When it was built, in 1926, it was the largest single span
structure in the world, extending 8,291 feet from portal
to portal. *Above* is shown Cemetery Hill, Gettysburg,
Pennsylvania.

**Symbols of the modern, technological age, electricity
power lines stretch into the far distance near Niagara
Falls, in New York State** *above.*
   **Reminiscent of a different age is the tranquil scene
at misty Loon Lake, also in New York State.**

The graceful 1000 Islands Bridge *facing page* spans the
waters of the St. Lawrence River in New York State. The
border between Canada and New York State is formed by the
Niagara River, with its mighty falls *above* which take on a
totally new appearance when held in the icy grip of
winter.

Illuminated by changing, colored floodlighting, two views
facing page and above **from the observation tower, of the**
might and immensity of Niagara Falls, New York State

Sand cliffs, with grass and scrubland *above* at deserted
Nauset Beach. In the distance stands the isolated Nauset
Beach Lighthouse, Cape Cod. With the distinction of being
the oldest of the Cape's attractive towns, Sandwich *facing
page* is famous for the colored glass that was made here in
the 19th century.

Overleaf left: a typical covered or 'kissing' bridge at Blair,
New Hampshire. *Right* is shown The Pool, in New
Hampshire's foremost scenic attraction, Franconia Notch, a
deep valley set between the Franconia and Kinsman
Mountain ranges.

Seemingly endless sandy beaches are just one of Cape Cod's many attractions, *facing page and above.*
Overleaf: **colored clay formations at Martha's Vineyard** *left* **and Marconi Beach, Cape Cod** *right.*

A blue and purple landscape lies under a winter sky as the dark shape of Mount Ethan Allen rises on the horizon *above*. A hanging veil of mist shrouds Vermont's Green Mountains *facing page*.

Overleaf: early-autumn leaves carpet the lawns and sidewalks at Vermont's Woodstock *left* and at Deerfield, Massachusetts *right*

279

As trees reluctantly shed their rustling foliage a patchy
covering of early snow coats the New England woodland
scenes *these pages*, warning of more severe weather ahead.

Vermont's trees, mountains and roads encrusted with a layer of snow and frost *above.* A slight thaw, or the wind shaking the branches of the trees, soon releases them of their burden and they stand green against the white of the surrounding landscape *facing page.*

Overleaf: **Water makes its way over and around rocks in the beautiful New Hampshire countryside.**